I0201323

Dear Mr. Cosby,

-

Katherine Elizabeth

Copyright © 2014
Katherine Elizabeth Eastvold

All rights reserved.

ISBN: 0988560151
ISBN-13: 978-09885601-5-4

To the man himself
above and below.

A hero is someone who has given his or her life
to something bigger than oneself.

Joseph Campbell

DEAR MR. COSBY

-

CONTENTS

1 PILOT PRESENTATION

Pilot Presentation
Season 1, Episode 1

—

Dear Mr. Cosby,

You don't know me and I, even though it feels like I do right now, don't know you. But I have to write you. Even if you never get this letter, I have to write you.

I have been told in the past that you have felt forgotten by us, the nation. I heard or read that somehow, in the craze of the late 90's and really, the haze of those first internet days that were the early 2000's, that you thought we had forgotten you.

I remember thinking how crazy that was, every time I heard it. How in the world could we ever forget you? How in the world could anyone ever take back those years from you? Deny you the inheritance of your good and plentiful harvest? It always baffled me- made me scratch my head.

In the end I always shook it off. "*Hollywood,*" I would think, "*Hollywood is such a sick crowd. Only they could make him feel that way.*" Because, let's face it, *Entourage* gives Hollywood such an amazing face-lift, doesn't it? In reality it rewards the corrupt and the perverse so much more than it does the hard work of the deserving.

The drugs that were tossed out on sets then are now handled and dispensed by studios as a way of controlling their assets (a.k.a. "people") now, and the sexual depravities portrayed on *Law & Order: SVU* are merely the trading cards parents know and willingly trade to see their surnames portrayed in a small rushed film-credit, never mind a silver screen.

No, I've known for years now that the only thing similar to a star in Hollywood anymore is the flash created by any of the photogs and the blackened gum-encrusted ones more people throw cigarettes on than take a picture next to.

And if I know these things, then I know that you know them even better. In fact, I bet you see much more of the good in Hollywood than I do. You're able to suss out the good from the bad and know a bad lie when you hear one.

So I've always shrugged the idea off, Mr. Cosby, that you could ever believe we've forgotten you. I've chalked it up to the press's love of sensationalism, shock value and disbelief. Because what could possibly be more shocking, right? The thought that we, a nation who hands-down adored you, watched you break records, boundaries and demographics with wild admiration and enjoyment rarely ever seen since, could ever *forget* you?

So I dismissed the idea. I knew you were too smart to buy it. You knew what it was when you heard it - the media's burning desire to shock us with the greatest untruths imaginable or simply some of Hollywood's old nay-saying and jealous gossip born from their sick needs to bring down someone who had seen all of their own dreams come true... and then some. So I shrugged it off.

No Mr. Cosby, I never obeyed that first thought of mine that always appeared first, *"Man, I gotta write him and set him straight!"* Because the next thought was always, *"What the heck, Katherine? It's not like he actually believes any of it..."* So I never wrote you.

Until today.

Because today I watched your first episode for the first time since it last aired some 20 to 30 years ago. I never knew it was available until today and when I did, I most hungrily and greedily devoured it! And now... it is over. And I sit.

I sit in absolute astonishment.

You did a lot more than entertain us, Mr. Cosby. You hypnotized us on the deepest levels. I am proof.

Dear Mr. Cosby, I want to tell you what it was like, watching your first episode- that first Pilot. I want you to hear it straight from me. I don't want anyone ever, *ever* diluting this for you. I want you to hear it straight, straight from me, a viewer that was a young girl when she first met you, and who is now, after seeing this first episode, suddenly deeply grateful for having met you.

Let me set the stage.

First, I am a writer. I didn't always write. It is a rather recent discovery, but I was clearly made for it. Teachers approached my parents for years begging them to build, develop and unleash this talent of mine, and for that very reason it was beaten out of me.

But they were unsuccessful. It took a good deal of surgery to recover, but recover I did, and a writer I am. And while I was healing, learning how to write again, I also learned a good deal about what it means to be a writer, and what traits are quite common among them.

Strange habits of mine were finally put into focus, placed in the puzzle of my whole picture, rather than on the set, neglected and ignored.

One of those pieces looks like this: when I love a show, or any piece of work or art, creative or otherwise, I tend to leave it be. I look at the canvas... alone. I don't research the painter. I don't look into their story - I just *look*. I study, examine and sometimes tenderly love upon that which they created.

Oh, I love documentaries and the realities of writers and I dearly love, love, love history. But there are some works that I just find to be better left untouched. Especially while the story is being told.

I cannot *stand* to be told an ending beforehand, much more so than the average Joe. I mean, I really, *really* can't stand it. And when a show is poorly written, then I can't stand it even more. I am shocked at just how blatant the bravado is of these television writers of late.

They are so inconsistent, so willingly to pretend that the last season or the last story or the last given reason just... doesn't exist! A character is thick, strong and demented on day three and on day four they are suddenly slender, tall and charming. That person died? Ope! Nope! Not anymore! And heck... we don't need to address it, do we? Nah... let's just keep writing.

I swear, sometimes I think the word "story" has been deleted from the dictionary altogether. But enough about that. My point is, I have learned that the reason we no longer watch television and the reason we hardly ever feel a trip to the movie theater is ever worth a couple bucks, is because we love *stories*.

We love a beginning, a middle and an end that all make sense. We love it when an actor's narcissism is actually veiled by their acting and we believe in what we're seeing on screen - whether big or small.

And because of that love for story, I protect the good ones at all cost. For example, the AFI's Top 100 of the last century (the one published on the millennium) introduced me to *The Sting*.

I loved it. I loved it all. I ate it up - yum, yum, yum, and though Google had already been introduced by then, I had no desire to learn anything! anything at all to do with its production, cast, etc. I swear, I don't know anything about Robert Redford, simply because I'm such an incredibly huge fan of all of his work. (Thank you AFI!)

And when I finally watched some of the best writing on this earth in *Homeland, Breaking Bad,* even *The Wire* and absolutely yes! *Galaxy Quest,* well - then I became a rabid dog - daring anyone to even *try* and tell me something about the backstory. No one even dares anymore. My friends have learned well.

That's because I have finally identified this little 'trait' many writers have, and have nurtured it and grown it and learned to love and protect it. But before I knew about it, it was still in me, even as a young, young girl.

And I never knew this about me - that it was in me all along - alive and thriving even in my young tortured youth - I never that until today - now - after watching your very first episode.

You see, as I watched it I found myself being torn up inside, here, there and everywhere! "*But wait... what? I thought there was a step there??? At the doorway. I could've sworn there was a step there!!! Aaargh! It's killing me! Why do they keep walking to the door like that? It's not supposed to be flaaaaat!*

Oh my heck, what's wrong with me? Why would I remember a thing like that??? And why do I even care so much?!? Oh and wait... wait! I remember the couch differently too! Hey Nick (nudge-nudge), hit pause. Babe, do you remember the couch that way? Wasn't it different???

And the stairs! I just KNOW the stairs were over the top on that side!!!"

And that's when all the memories came flooding back. All the scenes that I had memorized, locked away down inside of me in this special box marked "good memories" and "Cosby," that I didn't know even existed.

And I watched as the kids actually acted like real kids and the parents actually acted like real parents, and the marriage played out like an honest marriage. I marveled at the humor, marveled at the freedom and marveled at how my own life, 30 years later, mirrored much of what unfurled on that screen.

And that's when I knew. I suddenly knew - you were some miracle of a life vest that was thrown down to me from above. I didn't know it until today. But all the markers are there. I never did write you. I never did research you. I never ever tried to touch your show, learn about it or ever desire to know the drama or the stories behind those onscreen stories I'd come to memorize so completely.

Dear Mr. Cosby, today I learned that you were a big part of my life. So much of my childhood is painted in dark and light grays. Rare food, rare water, much blood and less love. Work instead of chores, dark instead of light - I just don't remember anything resembling the word "child" when it comes to the word childhood.

So it's no surprise when you hear that we weren't allowed to watch television. We weren't allowed radios or walkmans. What is shocking, really, is that you made it into our home.

I don't know how you did it. Maybe it was because it was set in New York and my mother hated California and missed New York very much. Maybe it was because my father's family who all lived within blocks of us all watched it, and if he was anything, he was a performer, born out of a need to convince them he was truly good - that everything was fine - that when it came to his kids, seeing was definitely not believing.

So one of them or both of them made your show mandatory. The very first show we ever watched that wasn't a cartoon. The very first show we ever gathered as a family to watch. The very first show we ever saw every single week. Our very first television tradition. We all gathered and we all watched, every single week. Oh thank God.

Thank you, Jesus. Thank you, Mr. Cosby. Because I have always said, always known since my studies in college and as a teacher, that parents have absolutely the most power in a child's life. They have the #1 influence over their children's future. What happens before birth to the age of 4 is sealed and written in them, waiting to unfurl with gusto and achievement once we take to starting our own families.

Oh, we can override them if we want. We can re-write the programs, yes, but just as it took blood to write such things, so shall it take blood to undo them. And I paid that price. I did it. I took the challenge and won. So here I am, getting to write to you, getting to say:

"You! You had power in my life beyond my parents. When they were gone you were left, and look at me. I've mirrored your writing, your love, your passion. I have your memories etched in my own. You made me laugh when no other laughter was to be found and you gave light when there was little to be had. Look at me, Mr. Cosby. I am all light, now, Mr. Cosby, and I love and have loved your show.

I love Claire, and oh dear! My husband knows that look. And I love Rudy. Oh dear, I remember that moment. And I love that story. Holy cow, I remember exactly how it ends. I know exactly how they all end! How is that possible? Oh, and how I love Vanessa - what an amazing actress. She nailed us older siblings to the very beat. I think I was like her as a child. And this scares me. It keeps making me me scared for her. I feel red, shame and danger for her. But you didn't beat her. Didn't question her. Just... *fathered* her? Is that what that looks like? Is that possible? Is who I am, deep down inside, worthy of the love of a healthy father?"

And here is the answer that you wrote on the screen:

"Most assuredly, yes. More than that, and in between. "

Dear Mr. Cosby, thank you... thank you *so* much... for writing to me.

Dearly and Truly,
Katherine

2 WHIRLWIND ROMANCE

Goodbye Mr. Fish - Claire's Case
Season 1, Episodes 2-19

—

Dear Mr. Cosby,

My, oh my, oh my! Am I *ever* in a whirlwind romance with *you*! I'm not done yet with Season 1, but whew! Nick and I are sure making it through fast! We haven't been like this since the releases of the Harry Potter books. We learned then that if we bought the books, we would each cheat and keep reading ahead without the other. We were terrible at it!

So that's when we learned about audio books, and they kept us honest, especially when they were still in cassette format. It was really hard to cheat when you couldn't get back to where we'd both left off together with the refined precision required to keep one of us off the scent of the crime.

Oh, yes, this is very much like then. Luckily Amazon's

Instant Video gives a bar to mark exactly how much we've consumed. I could cheat, I suppose, when he's off at work (lucky me, the joy of working at home!), but 10 years of marriage has proven that it is much better to wait and eat your show greedily together instead of apart. Time can do that.

So we have spent the last few days "binging" on your show, as Kevin Spacey likes to call it. I suppose he would know, with Netflix and all, but he's on my "crap list" for practically single handedly bringing back the "C" word for women. So forget him. Let's talk about why Season 1 is binge-worthy at all.

Well, first of all, everything that was out of whack for me in your Pilot Presentation, which we've gone back and watched a few times to compare, study and enjoy (I enjoy comparing changes and wondering why they were made - what the network might have said, or what you would have wanted instead and why, etc, etc. I may not look that stuff up, but I can't help but love studying the work itself!)

So we're much further in now. And yay! The steps are back by the doorway closet! I wasn't crazy! And woo-hoo! The tall staircase it right back where I remembered it. Denise is gorgeous and with all the fashion flares, I suddenly understand why I loved her character so much. I missed her so when she was gone. I realize now that I watched her very closely and I also know why now.

Then there's the sisters who actually fight - like, really, truly do fight! Just like we all did back then. Good heavens, there's a difference between the fighting between siblings then and the fighting there is now. But the chaos of the honesty on the show regarding the subject just made me feel at home... made me feel like safe somehow.

Oh! And the episodes! The whirlwind romance of the episodes for me! I knew the endings of every single episode before they happened. No - it's more than that - I knew the exact *choreography* the actors would do within the episode... before they would do them! I keep smacking Nick's arm in excitement:

"Remember this?! Remember this!?! Theo's about to--" and my husband kept saying, "Do you want me to pause it again?" Ah yes, the joys of watching these shows. I swear, we haven't laughed this hard in so long!

And you know what else? Nick and I are not even in the same generation. He is a whole generation behind me and you know what? He remembers the show too, and he relates to it, right alongside me. I'm amazed really, at the marvel of it - how we could be so far apart, from such different families, but share in this one thing together from our childhoods.

And I can't help wondering! Wondering how often these episodes played, how impossible it seems for me to remember every movement, line and nod of the head you guys make in this season. I love it, I love it, I love it all.

I look at the dates of when they first aired and I wonder if it took a while to get your Pilot off the ground

- if previews and more previews and other previews were again made of the episode, to sell it and massage it into audience after audience - to build it into the makings of a full show.

I don't know. I don't care. I'm just basking in the glory that is Season 1 of *The Cosby Show*. Exactly how long were you on? How many years? How many episodes??? I can't believe I remember so much of all of it. You must have been both my rock and my muse all those years, because I can tell, my body truly fed on each episode.

Who doesn't remember Theo's earring, and the pas de deux that took place between father and son in *Independence Day*- no words needed, just pure hilarity at the truth of it all. It makes me think, actually.

All these comics lately say that everything is funny, even rape jokes. They stand by each other, as each digs themselves deeper and deeper towards the pit of hell.

And I've always thought in my head, when I hear their words of support in response to queries about a disgusting pun, *"No, that's not true. It just means you're a bad comic."* Because I've always been told that the sins of such foulness only occur at the hands of the least talented.

The truly talented don't need to dig around in the dirt. The truly talented can make anything funny. If Shakespeare is still funny hundreds of years later, then nothing is ever too overdone to be done again. It's just how you do it. If you can't, you don't have the talent.

Your episodes prove that to me all over again. From comforting a daughter who is sick, to hitting on your wife in public, to sisters helping out brothers in ever-conspiratorial whispers, to sons wanting to look "def" for their school dance dates... every moment is a precious commodity unwasted.

The funeral in *Goodbye Mr. Fish* was no different. It's iconic for a reason. And every adult can relate to moving on more slowly than their child - making a small difficulty into a large one.

We all mean the best. We all live the life. And that's the palette you used. Only genius can make timeless jokes with it, such as the ones we are rolling and reveling in here. Thank you for each of them. I hope you didn't have to smash any Nerf bats on top of the corporate/network types' heads to get the green light on any of these, but if you did, Nick and I are living proof that it was well, well, *well* worth the fight and that you won.

All the way around.

Back to the Show,
Nick & Katherine

3 ARE WE CRAZY?

Denise's Decision
Season 2, Episode 22

—

Dear Mr. Cosby,

Somewhere in the middle of Rudy's bike lessons, I asked Nick to pause the show and said: "I feel like we're watching our future!"

And it wasn't because of our age, or because of the home or because of NYC, which we, by the way, we were perfectly fine with being portrayed by laminate backgrounds. When the writing and acting is that good, such simplicity is rather charming, actually.

No, we felt it was our future because of the rather "real," for us, yet humorous debate over Rudy's lessons: Mom vs. Dad. As I write this, I realize that it is very possible, most probable actually, that you did not intend these scenes to be real at all. They weren't meant to mirror precisely a day in our actually lives, today or

15

tomorrow.

You were writing a show. Creating a comedy. You intended them to be humorous. Comedic. Period.

That would make perfect sense. The show was a sitcom after all - a comedy - a show. And a show, by definition, implies "a piece designed to entertain." But I suppose I forgot all of that side of things, the entertaining and the humor... *Oh, right! They are simply jokes.* Lines designed for one purpose: laughter.

But I have to confess - I just haven't thought of these shows as entertainment for a long, long, long time. I've been watching these episodes as social commentaries, art, tools or insights for the road ahead. That wasn't my mindset as a child, I know that, but I've changed a great deal since then, and watched our society dip dangerously low.

And so I think of these things quite often, especially when it comes to the media. They no longer inform or entertain us, but train us... Train us to be alcoholics, codependent and either someone's foot rug or someone's bully.

Every Disney channel show for young kids has them drinking out of "single and ready to mingle" red cups in their hands at every waking moment. Frat party mentalities are no longer portrayed as a "phase" in life, but a way of life - from childhood to adulthood.

Pregnant women are pitied because they can't drink and now, oh Holy Lord, the glory of the cigarette is back. The last "truth" commercial I saw was in Canada.

And the little college town I recently moved to is a permanent marijuana smoke house. You can't live within blocks of the homes they rent, lest your lungs be filled with the stuff daily.

Parents just shrug their shoulders, defeated. Even the FBI is letting in the hackers who use it because they say that, "the kids grow out of it eventually." Um. No. Not anymore. This isn't the 70's. This is the "1/3 men are pornography addicts and 1/4 in women are too" culture. Those not addicted? They just don't have fiber optic internet yet.

Ah yes, I think of these things all the time when it comes to today's "media." I meet parent after parent who feel like they can't say "no" to their children's unhealthy patterns, simply because they are all portrayed as "normal" on every screen they turn to. "*Oh no*", the media says, "*marijuana isn't being legalized everywhere because it's too expensive to house all the offenders anymore. No, marijuana is actually a great drug and we're just opening our eyes to that fact now.*"

Sigh. Because a 'high' society is a drunk society. And drunkenness leads to bad decision making. And bad decision making leads to $$$$$. Plus even more $$$$$. And then a little more $$$$.

In fact, just give us ALL your $$$ and we'll call it even, okay?

And they wonder why the middle class is dead. And I realize why it still existed in the 80's. Your show. Pretty darn hard to deny it, don't you think? Remember, it was a "material world," back then, but somehow we kept it all in balance. Heck, we even saw the Berlin Wall fall, and for the first time, the country learned what it was like to live without the fear of complete nuclear annihilation in a long, long time.

But that threat kept us aware - kept us humble. How very different the threat of nuclear war felt compared to today's terrorism. It makes the generation gap only that much larger.

So these are the eyes I watch your show with. Perhaps we'll blame such eyes on my education at UCLA. I did major in the very art of analytic thinking. But because of that, I went on to empower and change the lives of students - training them with the same tactical eyes, the same awakened outlook that would space them and propel them, especially on those inner-city streets.

I taught my large and overflowing inner-city classroom students to never take a piece of writing, a commercial or a "show" at its face value. I taught them that every single piece of literature they read had an author behind it, a creator. I taught them that behind every commercial they saw was a company or corporation, trying to say and/or sell something. Behind every play, a writer, trying to instill or impart something to their readers.

And I taught them that all of these things - art, commercials, movies and shows - that these creations were always, always, *always*! made as a means to sell an idea, thought or emotion to each of their consumers.

So perhaps you were doing more than making us laugh with your show, Mr. Cosby. Perhaps you really were saying more. Maybe you did want to paint us a picture of possibilities and of hope - that the day-to-day raising of our kids is something we all share, and here's how we can laugh alongside it?

When I told my husband that watching this episode was like watching our future, perhaps this is what you hoped for? I do wonder... Because I'm scared of raising a family. Kids screaming at high pitched volume and length - getting whatever whenever they ask for it. I feel so alone when I watch them - I want to actually raise them instead of keep them, you know?

I want them to be ready to go out into the world able to handle whatever whenever it happens... on their own, as adults - healthy and strong - both physically and mentally. I don't want them to need me morning, noon and night when they are in college. I want them to explore, enjoy and expand... but no one seems to want that anymore... so I feel like what I want is impossible.

And then I see your show, and this episode, and I realize, "*I'm not crazy. I can raise kids. This is exactly what we would do. This is* exactly *how we would love... Maybe - just maybe - it is possible...?*"

———

You see, you've reached us at a very pivotal time. Nick and I hope to start a family in the coming year. Unmentionable and dark issues have prevented us thus far, but we have finally turned a corner and hope to begin. This, however, means that we have had nearly a decade's worth of an amazing friendship, partnership and marriage. Marrying your best friend is a hot thing. Marrying a younger man is a hot thing too. (Sorry. Is that TMI for you, Mr. Cosby? I can't figure out if you're my future, my mentor or myself up on that screen! But the show makes me feel like saying anything is safe.)

Anyhow, without children, we've had the luxury of laughing everyday. People constantly think we're newlyweds, and when I've asked around through my vast array of friends, classmates, students, teachers and readers, the resounding reply seems to be, "That all ends when you have kids."

Wow. We weren't ready for that reply.

So I want to thank you for giving us the gift of seeing the kind of laughter and the kind of wit we use with each other, play out in the area of children. We know it's just a show. We know real life is much harder. But the reality of our own lives is being lived out on your show - it's uncanny.

I love my husband. We flirt. We flirt to music like Heathcliff and Claire. We flirt in the kitchen like Heathcliff and Claire. We flirt through our good day, our bad days, our jobs and, well... just a great deal of our days.

Some people don't like it. Some even hate it. My mother said Nick would leave me because of the way I flirted with him. Others flinch and think we're "giving each other a hard time." Or, "giving each other crap." Nick and I call it being honest and open with each other, but...

There's a part of you that listens, you know? It's hard not too. There's a bit of shame attached to it, especially around those parental people - the ones with the word "no" written all over their faces.

So in the past we've wondered... "*Are we crazy?*"

And maybe we are. But we're not alone. Even if they are characters in a cast. Because we're finally seeing our own reflections in a couple on a hit TV show from twenty years ago. And because it's a hit, and because it's genius... well, we feel pretty darn proud of ourselves. For the very first time.

Why?

Because we didn't get to be like Cliff and Claire on accident. We did the work. Oh, did we ever do the work. And you know what? The other people, the vast majority of people we meet...they always want to know why we're so happy all the time. They may not trust the way we work, but they sure do like its results.

We laugh. A lot. We fight. Hard. We love. Love, love, love, love. Yes, he massages my feet. And yes, I tie a bow around his favorite book after keeping the house quiet for him to sleep after a hard night's work.

We are all over Heathcliff and Claire. They make us feel normal. They make us feel proud of the work we've done to get to where we are.

And now, hopefully, they will make us feel the same

way when we teach our kids how to ride a bike. Because every time I dream about it? That's exactly what it will look like. Though *he* will be on the porch and *I* will be grabbing on to the bike seat. He will teach her better and I will just have to deal with it.

And love every single second.

Truly Thankful,
Katherine

4 THE MARCH

The March
Season 3, Episode 6

—

Dear Mr. Cosby,

The end of *The March* touched me today. I was not ready to "watch another one" like we so often do after an episode ends. We were both touched, soothed and even fed a little when he started singing. I can still hear his voice. It echoes in my heart and in my soul.

You were not scared to end an episode that way. You wanted to and so you did. And I believe that paid off for America.

Because as I sat there, hearing Martin Luther King's march being revisited, I remember thinking, "*Wow. No wonder I couldn't wait for Thursday to watch this show.*" It was like church for my little young soul.

There are only two shows that I remember the days of as a child, and yours was one of them. I don't remember

23

if my parents let us watch on the night of, or if they used a taped copy or not. I just remember that the family would gather to watch it. We never gathered as a family, more than once a week to watch anything. Once yours was over, it took a couple of years for them to find one again, and when they did, I realize now, it did not "feed" me like yours did.

There was a time I might have thought this was because of my age... that I watched yours when I was younger, which means I might have been more impressionable. Or perhaps I just liked comedy aspect (the next show was Jean Luc Picard territory). But I am much much older now, and I have seen much much more than you can imagine. I know now that *The Cosby Show* was, for me, my weekly bread.

I needed to see a healthy and whole family. I needed to see them live. I needed to see them love.

Like I've said in previous letters, the marriage the show revolves around (at least the one portrayed in the for the first two seasons), is such a mirror to my own relationship with my husband, neck-locks and laughter and the basics galore, that I can't help but wonder if you had a hand in the making of us.

I can't tell you how many times I've had to stop an episode while we're watching so I can just sit there in awe, especially when we first started watching them. I couldn't believe that what I watched as a child had come to fruition in my own adulthood. I'd think, "*How is this possible? How am I able to sit here and watch, well, us up on that screen?"* Minus the five kids actually. I would like to have four. I wonder if we'll flirt as much then? Hmmm... Probably. I don't see his love of Jazz ending any time soon!

Anyhow, Mr. Cosby, I have to say, we stop the episodes a lot actually, to talk about it or discuss it at times, which again, supports the weekly 'bread' theory. My weekly bread. Oh, how much you must have fed that little growing girl! I thank you so much for it.

I'm again wondering how in the world you got through to my parents??? How did you convince them to make your show a part of our lives... of my life... when our own home was so different? I am in awe that they let us see it. Hmmm... Perhaps it was clean enough, or the local Parish listed it as a 'safe' program for kids to watch? Oh please, we didn't get *Little House on the Prairie* or *The Brady Bunch*. Nope. It was a miracle. Nothing short of a miracle. I am convinced.

Or... Maybe it's because good stuff is just good stuff. And everyone likes good stuff. Or in this case, great stuff is just great. You, somehow, ascended the gates of heaven and whispered in God's ear and he turned on the light in my parents' house. Hmmm...

In the end, I don't care what caused the minor miracle that gave me, young Katherine, so small, wounded and worn down to the thinnest of papers, the ability to watch you and your show and all the wonderful, loving actors in it, who were brave enough to do what they did for all of us. I just embrace it.

And I've learned more about what you did. I know now that *The Cosby Show* was simply a 30 minute safe-haven from hell for me. It was this warm glowing ball that I now call hope. It told me such saving words as:

"What you know and have experienced is not all that there is on this planet. There are different families out there. Different moms, different dads and different siblings. They are different ways of touching. Ones that make more sense. There are different ways of scolding, fighting and talking to and with your parents. There are parents who want to listen, homes that want to welcome and lives that have more freedom."

I remember staring at the art on the walls of the Huxtable home, soaking them in, memorizing them. I drank in their colors, their forms, their feelings. I drew breathe from them. I watched the clothes each character wore. I drank in the earrings, the hair, the beauty and choices.

I remember vibrancy of Claire and how happy she was. Her profession and the education... oh! The education that you encouraged! College wasn't a joke - it was an expectation, a truth and a reachable accomplishment. That little girl dove into the walls of that home and explored every nook and cranny, believing it was all real - all possible.

I was a young child, and I was being fed her very first morsels of real *life*.

The nourishment was priceless, I now think, and I am sad that there is nothing out there for the lost children of

DEAR MR. COSBY,

today. I don't think anyone wants to reach out to them unless it is to prepare them to be a credit card carrying and using member of society who spends spends spends without thought of today, tomorrow or next week.

Oh the lost children. How I do yearn for them.

So I thank you, Mr. Cosby, for moving past the sitcom tradition of just making that one single episode a season that deals with serious issues like drugs, drunk driving, etc. Does that even happen anymore? I wouldn't know. But when the discussion of The March began in this episode, I knew you were feeding the nation.

Your show was already entertaining. The casting near perfection. The writing different and curvy. The entire premise and atmosphere, warm, welcoming and so inviting as to be addicting. We wanted to be in your house. We wanted to be in that family.

You could have kept it that way. You could have stayed and settled into success with pet lizards, fighting siblings and work struggles for even more than your eight actual seasons. But when I saw you go there once more, into a serious subject, barely into Season 3, I saw your intent.

You knew you had America. You knew they were in your hand. You knew this was a historic thing you were doing and you knew its potential. So you used it. I wonder who was on board with you? I wonder if it's something the networks hated. I wonder if the networks loved it. I wonder how the actors felt about it. I wonder what the press thought. And I wonder how you managed to keep all those voices out, and if you ever really succeeded at that.

It's what terrifies me most about writing - other voices landing in my head, distracting me from my God-given instincts, inspirations and discoveries.

However it happened, you used the platform you had to cement in history a record of the voices at The March. As Russell quoted Martin Luther King Jr., my stomach turned queasy at the thought that, had MLK been here today and given a speech, the vast majority of the audience would not have understood it. The diet of inhumanity at its basest level has ground us into a feeble heart that cannot bear to listen, but only be heard. Oh the twisted fate of technology. The grated irony that the young's ability to operate fancy touch screens trumps the elderly's ability to say, well, anything... not their memories of the Holocaust, not the lessons they've learned in life, nor their thoughts on communication and humanity. Tsk tsk.

Mr. Cosby, thank you for educating me tonight. Thank you for doing it so often. Thank you for giving me a window into our nation's past. It may be painful as I compare it to our present, but it made me think of those I have shared such times with, much smaller though they've been. That spirit still lives, though secret and seeking in our nation's womb.

I loved, perhaps most of all, the song you brought to us, and such the right song and singer. As I listened to the words, I was struck with the fact that Martin Luther

King Jr. was a Reverend. Would a Reverend be able to give voice to a nation that way again? And with all the divisiveness between political parties, would such a massively diverse crowd like the one your show described ever be able to agree or enjoy themselves again? Together?

"Together we stand. Divided we fall..." If that really holds true, then our foundation has some deeply concerning cracks in it.

I've heard a friend say that we, as a nation, were more united during the days of your show. Perhaps that was because of the Cold War. I remember being scared of nuclear annihilation. I remember being very aware of that possibility. I remember some sleepless nights over it, as a member of a military household.

Perhaps, then, we were more united when we watched your show. Perhaps, back then, we did not find such poignant "hard issue" shows polarizing or controversial. Perhaps, back then, America watched it and was proud... proud of our heritage and that history.

Your characters say that their strongest memory was of how kind everyone was to one another, no matter what bus, what corner or what clothing they wore. That really struck me. I know it was one of our greatest days and I am so proud of our nation for being the kind where such an event could happen, and being the kind where such content was free to be aired on television at all, and even recognized and remembered.

And I'm glad you placed that moment in an episode.

KATHERINE ELIZABETH

You "let the people speak" once more. And by doing so you also fed us, the hungry. I can see her now, this little girl, sitting on the grey hard floor, in a corner with her bit of bread for the week. It was so hearty that it would last her a good long while, and make her weep with prosperity... more than two decades later.

Katherine

5 A NEW WORD

Cliff in Charge
Season 3, Episode 13

—

Dear Mr. Cosby,

I just finished watching *Cliff in Charge*, and there is a settled peace in the room. It's still, quiet - not warm, but calm... and... Right. It took me a while to figure out what the episode was about - there was no tragedy to be solved, no wrong to be righted and no quandary to unravel. I've loved the fact that the episodes, especially in Seasons 1 & 2, have been so simple - not contrived, not predictable, not "produced" like most sitcoms have become. They always seem to have floated on humor - as if you knew that humor was enough, in any form.

After a while I felt more structure coming, and I followed along just fine. Quality is quality. But this episode was different somehow. It was humor there, and then laughs here, then a special point made in the middle or end... well, I suppose that's not exactly true.

Because at the end of this episode, I still sit. The room is still quiet. The 'right' still hangs in the air, and my mind still holds the image of his hand on the door, closing it behind him... closing, and telling and loving.

It was there, at that moment, as he closed the door behind him - there was a pause, wasn't there? I know the audience began applauding before it, but I still felt as if there were a hold - a hanging in the air - a moment in the balance.

And that moment said, *"See? See here - this is what the episode was about."* The answer came there at the end for me, in that moment.

The episode was not about him, the grandfather. It was not about you, the doctor. It was not about Claire's absence or the challenges of familyhood or the trials of childhood. Instead, it was about love.

Love. I didn't see it coming, but it hit as sure a rain upon the sweet wet ground of pavement - love.

Not the kind of love I hear about anymore. I really feel as if this were the first time I ever encountered it. Is there a name for this 'love' you painted today for us?

When the scene opened, earlier in the episode, where Rudy had fallen asleep on her grandfather's chest, I said aloud to my husband, in rather stark enlightenment, "Our kids will never know that!"

He just paused, then nodded. It breaks us right in the air, knowing neither of our families are safe for our future children. But they will wonder. They will ask...

How do you handle such a thing? How do we bless our kids with that kind of love and safety? And I said to myself, "*We will find such family in others...*"

Because we will. Family has many colors. Ours will be a shade unlike most, but we will have a place for our children to rest their heads. I know it.

And I pray, I pray so dearly and so hard... I pray that I, that we, that you... have that new type of love I just discovered, here at the close of your portrait of it. I cannot pinpoint how you did it. I cannot pinpoint where and when the weave was woven, but I feel it. I feel it preserved in this stillness.

The inheritance of love. Father to son? Son to father? The moving parts that can move without changing the essentials? I want a name for this love that just unfurled like a soft flag before me, without my even catching it until now. I want a name for it. I want a house for it. I want my home, my father and mother and sons to know it.

But this love will have to come some other way. I don't know. I just desire it. Its peace. Its calm. Its knowing. And its unchanging. To say you are proud. To say you are proud. To say you are proud...

To tell a story, to give a name, to unlay that which came before onto the ground of that which will be traveled.

Family is a hefty story. Family is a hefty height - a subject to be cleanly broached. My family is broken. I have a hard time writing that, saying that, speaking that even! even with all that I say and all that I've said... I still have a hard time writing that. My family is broken. From drink, from sex, from monsters and from criminals. My family is broken. I don't want a mirror on the wall. I don't want to see all that they have done. I don't want to mouth out the words "molester" "rape" "kings" and "torn." I don't want to mouth out the cruelty, disease and crises that plagued us. But I will. Because I won't know that new word of love until I face it... If I face it, I can press it to the side, choose to put my feet forward and my past to the part.

I can have that love you so quietly brushed out for all of us. I'm not exactly sure how, but I am sure. Sure that I have the guts and the anger and the poise to knock it right into the place it should be and not where it was.

And to fight. I'm sure enough to fight. I want that peace that sat on Rudy's sleeping freeing head. I want that secret tickle that tucks her tight and secure. I want that freedom of the air she breathed in that moment of time, and I want a bedtime story that will rile me up, even at the age of 40, 50 and 60, and make me feel this still, still, quiet-calm still, that is Love. Only painted on tilt.

6 CONFLICTING REPORTS

Cliff's 50th Birthday
Season 3, Episode 20

—

Dear Mr. Cosby,

There's a big question that's been weighing on me during your Season 3, but I guess I was just hoping the answer would come, or that the desire would fade and disappear into the nights as we traveled on and on. But nope, I have to ask it!

But at first I have adore on you a little just once more about this last episode we watched, *Cliff's 50th Birthday*. It just really struck me how the show handled the issue of divorce. These Seasons of *The Cosby Show* have reminded me of the days when sitcoms always had that "important issue" episode, the one that approached difficult subjects, like drunk driving and abuse.

But today you handled the word 'divorce.' It's rarely talked about anymore now. I don't think many

Americans would venture to say divorce is a "difficult subject" that entertainment shows should or would address. I was watching an *EWW (Everything Wrong With)* video, if I remember correctly, on some Justin Bieber movie on YouTube (yes, I believe there are actually some movies that really deserve an *EWW* made about them! [But I could kick the creator, CinemaSins, for even daring to touch the *Wizard of Oz* and other movies that were actually good. Sins indeed!]). But as I watched the evil-Bieber, I found myself devastated by one single shot. And he wasn't even in it!

It was when three little young girls excitedly jumped up and down, saying, not that they wanted to marry him exactly, but that they wanted to be "one" of his many TBA wives, apparently. They giggled as they proudly named exactly which wife they wanted to be to the Biebs: Wife #1, Wife #2 or Wife #3!

I wanted to fall down. What has happened to the girls of today!? They don't even hope for a marriage to their dream man, just a shot at being a negative part of his life - a divorce and the pain that comes with it. *Our children* assume *they'll divorce!* They don't even try to *aim* for that, apparently elusive, shot at marriage!

What does this mean, actually? Does this mean they'll find your shows and these seasons as some kind of science fiction? Will my marriage to Nick really seem that strange to them? As if it were pretend or something?

Brrrr. I shiver.

But back to *Cliff's 50th Birthday*, which did approach

the subject of divorce with some respect and some seriousness. Here is what struck me when the episode was finally over:

You did not simply address the issue of divorce, did you? No. You also broached the issue of conflict - conflict between adults. And when you turned the camera upon the conflict, you didn't wash it in butter or slippery soap, so that there was no real stance or ground for the conflict to take its form. *Modern Family* has conflict woven so deeply into every fiber that each episode only ever resolves two or three threads of conflict, while having a hundred threads repeatedly playing out within the very nature of each character.

Watching it is sometimes wonderful, but I have to admit, I've never watched a single episode without flinching at least once. The slicing cut of a husband's insensitivity, the shaming snort of disgust for a daughter's use of her mind, undercuts here, undercuts there and they all smile and laugh at the end of an episode, while I find myself wondering exactly what it would take to get them to finally seek therapy...

Because conflict doesn't just lay there unresolved for all of eternity, does it? No. It's like a festering wound that grows slowly - especially in families. So slow, in fact, that it can go for years, spreading and expanding. And we can ignore it for a while. Oh yes, it turns other people off. Oh yes, we lose job opportunities over it or important relationships, because they can see that wound, loud and clear on you, but you're not going to face it yet. You don't want to. You'd rather go on. And roll your eyes at someone else - especially that person you usually vent to.

But here's what always happens, no matter what. That wound gets too big. It bursts, or it breaks and the infection flies everywhere and you find yourself crippled. Mass destruction. Chaos. Pain. Confusion.

But *Modern Family* doesn't portray any of that, does it? Ah, no. Because conflict resolution is healthy, and healthy people don't let go of their wealth easily, and that's great news for the owners who own everything. And of course, we as a society like to bury our heads now don't we? Because facing conflict, means facing the truth, and facing the truth usually means making some hard decisions or choices in our lives... and our culture no longer cheers for that, do they? "*No... If I have to deal with an abusive mother, then you have to too,*" each person feels, and so we receive no love, support or affection - never mind any TV time.

But you did something entirely different, didn't you? Your show did the exact opposite. You not only said, "Here. Here is conflict. An extremely difficult conflict," but then... you resolved it. Not by jokes. Not by sweeping it under the rug. Not by making it magically go away.

Nope. You portrayed the "adult" version. We watched on as the adults made decisions that would, today, are practically branded as sins:

- They (gasp!) acknowledge and face the conflict

head on.
- They are honest with their feelings.
- They are forthright about their opinions and emotions.
- They communicate with one another
- They (gasp again!) resolve the conflict instead of delaying it.

I love it. I admire it. I thank you all for it. You gave us such a great, yet funny, example of how things should be handled in a healthy world - even regarding the awful subject of cheating too.

Oh, how it's practically holy to me! The adults on the show acted like adults. How novel. Have you noticed how few adults on the screens these days actually act older than 3? A Bravo executive spoke about a woman they dismissed from one of their reality shows. When asked why they had let her go, he stated. "She was too human."

Huh. Thanks a lot. I never watched the channel again. Humanitarians need not apply.

Speaking of awkwardness, I'm finally ready to bring up that observation I was so mysterious about at the start of this letter. I hope you will excuse the intrusion. I hope you won't take offense, but I'm too wriggly about it - too irked - too curious - too hungry. So please excuse any impropriety on my part, especially because I wasn't there, but...

...What the heck is going on with Season 3!?! I mean, what executive, what person, what feedback, what stats, what - what - *what* was the reason for the big switch in Season 3!?! Where did Cliff go, and who is this guy taking his place? And why him? Why, why, *why*!

I can't help but believe you know exactly what I'm talking about. Let's see. Seasons 1 and 2 were smash hits. And in those seasons, we watched Cliff Huxtable be the equal partner in a marriage, with maturity and character, with wit and... well, patience? Yes. Love? Yes. Kindness, strength and ability? Exactly. More or less. And the same goes for Claire.

My point is, we fell in love with Claire and Cliff - the dynamic duo - who loved each other and loved their kids, suffered each other and suffered their kids. Smart, funny and smashingly fantastic!

Soooo.... why does Season 3 suddenly turn Cliff into a sad waddling dog with long floppy ears and a tail between his legs??? I swear, at one point I turned to Nick and said, "What the heck! I think he's playing Eeyore!" (from Winnie the Pooh).

The entire premise of the show suddenly seemed to turn from "dad and mom making it happen," to "mom and kids taking pity on and making fun of dear old dopey dad." Man. We have had more than enough of that soppy story by now.

I doubt you started it, but someone did- the trend of making father's the brunt of everyone's jokes. I remember writing assignments in high school about the fall of the father in the eye of the media. Dad gets it wrong and mom gets it right. Dad's out of touch and ha, ha, let's laugh at him.

Dopey dad.

When the heck did that idea get started for such an amazing character as Heathcliff?

Aargh. But I have a theory. I so wish you could affirm or confirm it! I just can't help but think it's what I call the "Season 3 Blues." It's a term I've developed over time for a phenomenon and affliction I see hit shows go through, time and time again. Here's what I think happens:

1. A show gets started and when it airs, it becomes a huge hit.
2. People (people in the biz - execs, producers, artists) start talking about it and buzzing about it. They aren't part of the show, but everyone's talking, talking, talking, but nothing trickles down to the show yet because when they just start to talk, Season 2 is already being taped.
3. Then comes Season 3...

By Season 3 I know the movers and the shakers of the show have been hearing from their peers about what they think. And their peers are in absolutely no condition to speak, because they certainly had nothing to do with the creation of this hit show... But speak they do.

And do they give you hit-makers praise? Sort of. They say, *"Congrats!!!"* And then they always follow it but with, *"But..."* And it's those *bleeping* "but's" that cause all the trouble. Creators of the show start fixing what Just. Isn't. Broken! They respond to the complaints of the few despite the great feedback of the many.

I wish there was a cone of silence around every creator and/or artist of great things. People have an amazing ability to get in your heads, don't they? And they're even better at it now, when they don't have to be face to face with someone when they express their criticism. We are a culture of "mean when unseen." Blech. Good thing the law is finally catching up.

Anyhow, I'm just curious (okay, a little more than curious) as to what happened to Cliff and Claire in Season 3. I wonder why they don't flirt, why they don't giggle and why they don't shine. I wonder where the real Heathcliff Huxtable went, and I wonder if he's ever coming back.

I sure do hope so. I miss him so very, very much.

Over and out,
Your "enjoying being an adult" fan,
Katherine

7 Y2K

Hillman
Season 3, Episode 25

—

Dear Mr. Cosby,

As I watched Claire sing against the background of a full choir, the immense notes and floatations of *All Good Things* ringing so deep and sound, as they were supposed and meant to, I thought once again, as I have so many a time during these last three seasons, "*Wow. This would never be allowed on television anymore.*"

My mind, as it always does, enters the courtroom of the producer's office, or the network's headquarters, and I saw the argument, "*No, it's a Hymn - and hymns remind people of church or God or a higher power, all of which is off limits...*"

But this time my mind didn't get much farther than this. Because you weren't depicting a church. I mean, you were, in that you were actually in a chapel - no, you

43

were in a church. But I only know this because I've been there. Will you please pardon me as I take a sidetrack here? I'd really love to share this with you. It's so special to me...

The moment your cameras opened onto the large white booming hall of "Hillman's" graduation ceremony, I shot up and immediately hit pause. My husband is used to my sudden outbursts of inspiration, so he just calmly waited by, but I don't think he was ready for what I said next.

"That's it! That is the place!!" I waved my finger at the screen. "It has to be!" He just smiled and waited until my excitement could calm down enough for me to put more words to it...

"It's where Michelle and I went for the change of the millennium!!! In 2000!!!"

But that was more than he was expecting. His jaw dropped. His eyes super wide, he turned to fix them on the screen.

You see, he's heard the story a million times. Over and over he's heard it, because he wasn't there. I hadn't even met Nick yet, and it was a really, really important and very memorable time for me. Because way back in 1999, I knew only one thing about the change in the millennium - I wanted to be worshipping the Lord when the ball on this last century finally dropped, ushering the next one in.

Look, I came to the Lord on my own. Not by my family, not by my friends, but alone. And once I was

His, I delved in deep - started attending non-denominational Bible Studies, mission trips, classes, courses and even worked in church offices and in church leadership. I was in love, and so I did what my family taught me to do for the ones you love - work myself to the bone.

I eventually broke all of my bones in the process, leaving me without the ability to work anymore. There in that place, I learned it wasn't necessary, and I left such a life behind. But though I may have left the straps and bonds of duty behind, I never left Him behind. He had charted a new course for me - one that eventually led me straight to my husband and my calling as a writer and adventurer... as well as a few other key things. In short, He rebooted my system. Put me on a new path. I didn't see it. I didn't know it. I just knew I was broken and I loved Him.

And it's because of that that I found myself in "Hillman's" ceremonial ground. A few things had stuck with me from my days as an avid parishioner in college ministries that I actually really enjoyed doing - because I wanted to and not because I had to. One of these traditions was ushering in the New Year while singing what they call "praise and worship." These ministries would hold big gatherings and we'd come from all different corners of the state and different colleges, all different denominations, and we'd join hands and sing worship songs straight from the end of the old year and right on into the New Year.

It was our way of giving Him the first moments of our New Year. It was, I suppose, an offering of sorts.

As I said, I didn't bring the legalism of that culture with me when I left, but I did bring the heart of it. I related to it. I liked it. I enjoyed doing it. It really stayed with me. So as I saw Y2K approaching, I knew I wanted to be with Him when it started. A New Year came around a lot. A new millennia? Not so much.

But doing this was harder than I thought. Since I'd been steeped in that culture from almost the instant I was born-again at 15, I assumed *all* churches held that mentality. I thought, "*Of course every church will have a service that night - all I have to do is find one!*"

I was so, so, so! wrong.

Wrong, wrong, *wrong*. Ah, the follies of being so young that you can't imagine wanting to go to bed before the next dawn breaks. But I digress...

So there I was working at a dance convention that lasted for four entire days across the New Years weekend. My sister Michelle had driven up to join me for the night, also wanting to bring in the New Year this way. We joined a private party of our closest friends up in the hotel and stayed until it was time to go to church, an hour or so before the New Year, thinking we just a few minutes or so to find a church in order to enjoy a service. Unfortunately, this was pre-iPhone.

Looking back, I'm wondering exactly how we were that naive. We were so foolish! But out we slipped from the party that was just getting going and on to the concierge we went to point us to the nearest church.

But the concierge? He had only two church listings, neither of whom, to our great surprise, was holding any kind of service that night. We eventually found others who had services that day, but they were long, long since over.

What a shock this all was to us. I can't explain the panic I felt - the confusion. "*Why oh why would anyone bother going to a service at 6:30 pm on New Years Eve??? Why in the WORLD wouldn't they want to bring in the New Year this way???*" All this churned in my head, with spots of light finally cracking through my pretend world and giving way to some other world - one which I knew nothing about and completely misunderstood.

So what did we do? We headed out, determined to find a place of worship on our own... and we had very bad luck. Everything everywhere was dark. We ended up simply driving around looking for any church building with any kind of light on. Something. Anything!

And that's how we found Hillman. We saw great windows lit. Cars parked around. A side door opened. We immediately parked and ran. We were running out of time! But the front doors? They were locked! Every single one! But oh, we could hear them singing inside and we thought, "*Well, maybe they are worried about bad company wandering in?*" We didn't know, but I'll tell you this - we were so determined, so desperate, that we walked around the building to that open door we saw standing open.

It didn't look like a main door. It looked like the door to an office. But it was wide open with a huge box holding it back. And I'd seen some churches do that, hadn't I? For wandering guests??? Well. No. I hadn't yet, truth be told. But I had worked for so many churches by then that I knew we could somehow find our ways into the main chapel without disturbing anything.

"Maybe this is the main entrance for such a late night ceremony," we told ourselves. I mean, after all, what *did* we actually know after all? Isn't everything we had assumed so far been wrong?

And so, we ran in.

And it was too late. We couldn't take it back.

Many, many, many a time! has my husband heard the story. The story of my sister and I, two tall white chicks, teenagery in age and barely hatched into reality of the world, running and suddenly stumbling out into the great white open hall... not into a side hall like we'd hope, or a side door like we thought. Oh no. No, no no no no!

We popped ourselves right out onto the front stage. Just to the left of all the musicians who were playing. And right in front of the entire and huge congregation. We were stunned, blinked and stared with wide eyes. And they - the great huge hall - did the same. They looked stunned, wide eyed, as every single eye of the entire congregation turned upon us. And how could they not?

Not only did we shoot ourselves out of a canon into

their church service, so to speak, but... how shall I put this? Ummm... Let's just say that if they were to play a game of *One of These Things Is Not Like the Other*... then my sister and I would have had the great big hammer fall upon us. Because the walls might have been white, but the congregation wasn't. And we - we crashed their party.

Everything froze for less than a second. And since the worship team kept playing, I decided to keep running - straight on down the side aisle and into the back. We ran, ran as fast as we could, to the back of the church, and sat down in the last row... panting a big, but glowing. Not just from the red of deep embarrassment, but also from the gold glow of excited joy.

We sat there and sang and listened, even as we heard the fireworks blooming in the air outside. I think the Lord loves celebration and fireworks. But there I was, lucky enough to do what I had so wanted to do at the turn of the millennium. I was the one who so desperately wanted to spend that special night with Him, and you know what? They were the only other ones in all the area willing to do the same.

That was a big night for me. I've never forgotten it. I doubt the congregation has either. And ever since I've been left with the horrendous task of simply trying to describe that night to my husband.

And I've known, every single time I tried to tell him, that I was not doing those white walls justice. I was not filling the huge hall with the right descriptions - the passion of the people - their determination, their respect - their honor and their praise... I've always known I'd fallen short in my telling of the story

And then *Hillman* happened. And I hit pause. And I shouted in excitement to my husband and pointed at the screen and showed him the door we stumbled through, right in the very center of the screen - I can't believe I ever stepped foot in where you were, never mind treasuring a spot that I can only assume you treasured as well.

There is something so right in that place. There is, to be very sure, something holy there.

I won't lie. It took some time to start the episode again. I re-lived that night for my husband, showing him the doors we shook that were locked, the door we flew through bringing and entire community to a halt - and told him how they eventually relaxed, realizing that though we came unprepared, we came determined. We stayed through the New Year. I believe he preached well into the morning, but we did not make it. We made it long enough for the ladies in the back to help us slip out through more 'normal' channels, and for them to be kind to us - knowing we were kin... knowing we were part of a family stronger than this earth can bind and our eyes can see.

When we'd first entered, the edge sat on all their shoulders for a while, but that edge quickly faded, and my memory softly rests in the cradle of that large chapel that night. For what would I have had if not been for them? A lost moment under the stars? In a city that was not my home or my land? But I carry the year of Y2K bravely and soundly - happily in the arms of that night. I owe that church honor and I hold that church dear.

I am so glad I got to see it one more - thrice more! For I suppose I'd seen it as a child on your program, hadn't I? - and the circle has come round and complete.

I hope, dear Mr. Cosby, that this reminds you of that place. I hope, dear Mr. Cosby, that this brings a warm smile to your face. I really do hope, Mr. Cosby, that others felt the weight of that place - through the channel you provided, created and formed. I hope we've repaid the favor, Mr. Cosby - and perhaps I'll go see that place once more...

It's hard to pull back to that moment with Claire - singing against that choir. But I can and I will. I only want to say this:

The networks don't want to air such a scene again not because of the song and certainly not because of the church. You see, what you portrayed in this episode was really closer to reality than anything you'd done before. Graduation ceremony after graduation ceremony happens all the way across our land and across the world all the time!

Why don't we have graduation ceremonies depicted in our shows today? The networks love reality TV, right? So why don't we ever see these kind of realities depicted anymore?

I offer an answer: Education. Promise. Hope.

Education.

Education is the strongest antidote to the media. Education is the strongest force against saturation, impulse buying and impulse selling. Education fights advertising. Education fights drama. And drama keeps us muzzled - secret - bound - never to become free.

The networks, I propose, want your money, my money and everyone else's money. And education stands in their way. Purpose stands in their way. Responsibility stands in their way. If 1/3 men are addicted to pornography, and Hollywood employs less that 13% of its entire force with women, then isn't most of what we see written and developed by addicts?

Addicts attract other addicts - and at their very base core, they desire that thing they are addicted to, to be rewritten as not dangerous, not bad, not unhealthy... but normal. "*I brew my own beer. I know my wines better than anyone. Porn isn't naughty or bad, everybody does it. Girlfriends shouldn't stop boyfriends from watching it, they should encourage it. Marijuana isn't a gateway drug...*" Message after message today is more about teaching us to accept bad behavior instead of protecting ourselves from it.

So a graduation of such serenity and sincerity - such pride and such maturity and greatness - they might be happening all over the world, but not on television.

I believe that your episode may ring more of reality than any other show on television right now. But your episode, dear Mr. Cosby, this one called *Hillman*, would never be allowed.

I wonder, what do you think? Do you see the same woe and overflow? As you stand back and watch Hollywood swirl down the toilet? As all of the women's rights we so clearly achieved - that are reflected on your show and even in its credits - become stripped right away. As all the racism is now forced into us, hammered in by what they call "good TV." As they drip it into the veins of viewers in order to fuel their chaos? Do you believe we have become undone?

In *Hillman*, the resigning president of the college closes the episode with the following resounding speech:

> "...We need to move on to the future, perhaps 20 or more years, when you students will be twice the age that you are now, excelling in your chosen profession - and you are interrupted by a telephone call from a recent Hillman graduate who wants to meet with you in the hopes that you might share some of your wisdom with him or her... and maybe give him or her a job...
>
> Get in your car! And go to where he is and pick him up! Invite him to partake of a sumptuous meal. Share whatever you have. After all, that splendid young person is a Hillman graduate. And he should never, never, never! Walk alone."

It was an amazing speech, a resounding performance, and rightly so, they all stood up and cheered. Nothing could stop them! Pride of education and the power it brings could be felt far beyond the room we sat in. It was incredible.

But as He spoke of what a Hillman graduate might want 20 years down the line, I pulled up short. I counted on my fingers and realized that almost to the month, 20 years down the line of when this *Hillman* episode first aired... was the release of the iPhone. And though I did watch on, I couldn't stop myself from thinking, *"I'm pretty sure that's what that new Hillman graduate would have preferred - not the advice of someone 20 years their senior."*

Television had changed by then. The iPhone would have won. Do you agree? I wonder...

For what would happen if television went back to saying such things? That age really does breed wisdom, that youth can really learn more than they naturally do, that selflessness and giving back are worthy qualities instead of weak ones... what would happen? Then the youth might actually listen to their elders - the more experienced - the successfully employed - the ones who have been there before and made it through. What a nightmare for advertisers.

Because then they might actually learn, and in doing so, might actually acquire some Wisdom... the very poison of every market.

With love and good cheer, my dear Mr. Cosby,
Yours always,

DEAR MR. COSBY,

Katherine

P.S. Thank you so much for bringing back the lovely, playful and relatable relationship between Cliff and Claire for this episode. We very much missed them this season. It was SO good to see again... like coming home. Thank you. Thank you to whoever's decision it was to bring them back. Cliff and Claire... home sweet home. Thank you!

8 HOOK, LINE AND SINKER

Saying Goodbye

—

Dear Mr. Cosby,

It's been quite journey, compiling all these letters for you. I feel like I have relived so much in just a short amount of time. It's incredible, when you think about it. All the subjects you inspired in me, all the things that I have learned, all the memories that these three seasons have brought back.

Yet as much as I have written, I have not touched the surface of all that *The Cosby Show* has opened my eyes to. One of greatest areas of healing for me has been in way of "touching." Do we no longer air or exhibit healthy and loving touching in entertainment these days? I often complain about and take note of unhealthy touching I see.

Take *Game of Thrones*, for example. The opening credits animation makes viewers feel smart, cool and cutting edge, as do the amazingly detailed costumes and highly skilled actors. But at the end of the day, *Game of Thrones* is little more than an excuse to watch pornography and gore. Thirty buckets of fake blood per scene, nudity a mandatory costume for nearly every woman on the show at one point or another and worst of all... when the blood and the sex meet.

I have never had nightmares over a television show, but I guess there's a first time for everything. If you cut all those moments out, then you are left with about 10 minutes of good dialogue and action per show, and the whole season shrinks to a single hour a great TV. I think. But there's no way you can believe that should and/or would exist without rampant pornography addiction.

Stuff like that sets nearly every single humanitarian movement back a hundred years at least, if not more. (I seriously crack up when they use the lovely blond and her dragons for all the promos... anyone actually add up the minutes of her screen time? Total? Yeah.) What really sticks and won't let go is young children wanting their women cut up, gorged and swollen for sex.

Did you know the Queen of England visited one of the sets for *Game of Thrones*? What advisor told her *that* was a good idea??? What an incredibly damaging thing it is, to stamp her approval upon their brow. How many healthy children, women and/or men will suffer for that indescribable mistake?

Yet through *The Cosby Show*, I learned that I had missed something in the way of television trends. While the touching between humans on television turned more and more violent and criminal (*The Following's* first episode made me throw my hands up in the air. Exactly when did we start finding such things entertaining? Are we any better than the civilizations of a thousand or more years ago?), I realize now that healthy touching has been lost altogether.

What a shock it was, every time I saw Cliff holding Rudy or hugging his kids. What a shock it was to see Cliff and Claire kiss, soft punch and play-push. Even everyone kissing each other to say goodnight - I had a really steep learning curve.

Up until now, I thought I had a hard time with it because I'm a victim of sexual abuse by a family member. In those first few episodes I found this part of me instinctively protecting each child, wanting to put my arm between the adult and the child. Or perhaps it was due to my training as a school teacher. Touching kids was a huge no-no. We couldn't hug them, pat them on the shoulder, or even help them up. The only time we could touch them was to break up a fight. Oh geez - as I write that, good heavens - what a message that sends!

But I don't think it's just my training and my history. In California, I rarely saw anyone touching each other. Everyone has a phone in their hands. Shoot, there aren't even young couples anymore. No young people giggling and holding hands. As I think of it now, I remember that if anyone ever held hands, even at an amusement park, I'd always point it out to Nick.

DEAR MR. COSBY,

What's happened to us? What's happened to me? I loved your show when it first aired. I don't remember being squirmy for any part of it, touching or otherwise... but then again, I hadn't been assaulted yet. The abuse had not yet begun. Ah.

So this is it. I've learned something new. Again. Oh, Mr. Cosby, I hope this isn't all too much for you. I hope I'm not oversharing or overbearing or over-eager in any of these things. But you took a risk and did a show about Family. You touched on every edge, corner and crevice of Family didn't you? I cannot be the only one that was reached at so many levels.

Wow, the many who had the chance to watch you as and adult. Was it like this for them? Seeing a family actually working in ways we didn't know it could? Mirroring desires and feelings we thought were follies or fancies and giving us a goal to actual work towards? Do you think about that? All the families you touched, all the singles that watched and all the walls you knocked over and rebuilt within them?

I can't be the only one.

The press always talks about race when it comes to *The Cosby Show*. Wow. Race barely showed its face here in these letters. What does that say about the press? And I've heard disparity over the choice to portray a wealthy family. I watched and saw an educated and healthy family. Where was wealth they all complained about? Was the show about purchasing Versace? Were the storylines about the next trip to Rome?

I don't know, Mr. Cosby, but I think the loudest voices today are just that - the loudest voices. They scream the loudest. Cry the hardest. They throw a better tantrum than anyone else.

The voices you can't hear? They are the adults. The mature ones. The balanced ones. The ones who made your show a hit. The ones who tuned in and made Rudy, Vanessa, Theo, Claire, Cliff and everyone else a household name. And that didn't happen because of your color, your education or your economic status.

I think, if I have learned anything from reading these letters again, and watching your show again (one of the greatest gifts of my life, I now know and have proof), that you didn't become a part of our homes by breaking down enough barriers to make your way in... But rather because you did the opposite. We fell for you because you invited *us* in to *your* home and *your* set.

And we didn't come because you paid us. We didn't come because you charmed us. We didn't come because of any kind of marketing or trickery. No sir. We came because of the family you created. It was safe. It was loving. It was smart and it strong. In the end, we don't want our parents to worship us. We don't want to be told we're worthless.

We all want what your home provided. We all want what your home depicted. We all... man, woman, young, old, black, white, wounded, strong... watched and knew - this wasn't just a sitcom. It was an attainable way of life.

DEAR MR. COSBY,

And we bought it, hook, line and sinker. Thank God for that. Aaaaamen.

For the good times and the bad,
For making me laugh and making me cry,
For teaching me this and teaching me that,
For letting me write to you, here and now...

I will miss you,
Katherine Elizabeth Ever-Grateful Eastvold

TURN THE PAGE FOR YOUR
FREE PREVIEW!

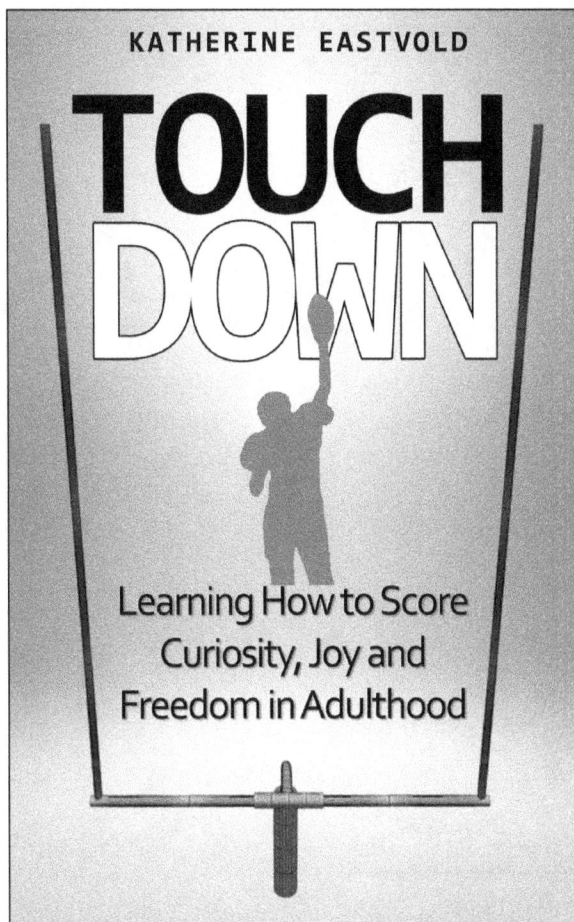

—

KATHERINE EASTVOLD

TOUCH
DOWN

Learning How to Score
Curiosity, Joy and
Freedom in Adulthood

FROM THE SAME AUTHOR AS DEAR MR. COSBY!

The following is a free preview of the author's groundbreaking book *Touchdown: How to Score Curiosity, Joy and Freedom in Adulthood*

1 GAME ON

Life is a game of football. People will tell you it's not. They will tell you to simply "envision" the ball crossing the goal line and your body will get you there, automatically, as if your mental, physical and emotional states can all become aligned, in sync and extremely powerful by this one simple act of focus.

Too many make it sound easy, painting a picture of you floating over the ugliness, craziness and chaos that is life and crossing over that goal post and landing, unscathed, uninjured and perfectly peaceful, on the other side of those large looming posts... happy, content and in a state of "win."

Yeah. It's not like that, is it? While our eyes are closed, focusing on that golden apple of a goal post down the field, a linebacker tackles us. What the? Then a bunch of other big guns jump on top of him. We are so shocked and startled that you.... yup, you guessed it... drop the ball.

Ah. It's such a nice picture, that peaceful floatation device of a dream, isn't it? It takes no prisoners. No war. No violence. No conflict. No devices. It only requires us to keep an eye on what we want, not what we can't have, what's sneaking up on us, coming at us and most definitely not on the very real road blocks that are uniquely designed for each of us.

(You do know we have designer road blocks, right? One of a kind, high end, extremely effective road blocks for each of us. For free too! Prada did a really great job on them.)

But while the programs, meditations and techniques all train you in ways to rise above it all and, well, skip the crap, so to speak, we still seem to have a really difficult time actually doing this without disconnecting all ties to the relationships and world around us.

It's really hard to stay "above" it all for very long. We leave our loved ones behind, thinking we have the answers and they don't yet. We become so focused on ourselves that we simply lose empathy or compassion for others.

I don't understand the whole "being in the now" notion. It sounds still, stiff and rather alien. I rarely meet people who are both dedicated to their "pictures" of what they want and are also full of joy, freedom and curiosity. In other words, I haven't met a lot of people who've either danced on the other side of that goal line, making a major touchdown, or who are making a run for it, free and clear of any other opposing team members - all because of their ability to float. Or stay still. Or be "in" any certain kind of state of "being."

Wait. Strike that. I haven't met *any*.

The truth is that we are all down there on that field. And it's impossible to win the game without skills. Life skills. We have to have a great offense and we have to have a great defense. Period.

It's not pretty. It can get dirty. If we don't prepare, don't see the play, get caught unawares too often, we move farther and farther away down the field from success and our end zone. It's harder and harder to get that ball back down the field for a touchdown.

But we can. There's always a way. Sometimes it's luck. Most of the time it's skill. And luckily our four quarters are a lot longer than 15 minutes, though we really don't have a halftime, as much and as dearly as we may desire one.

Sometimes I think the New Age philosophies trick us into thinking we can win the game during the halftime show, when we are alone and no one is looking. I'm okay with that. I don't agree with it, I wouldn't necessarily ever promote it, but I will always let others make their own decisions for themselves. Go where you please.

I'm here for the ones who *don't* feel it connects the dots for them. I'm here for the ones who know life is down there on a field - who know it's a game - who know it's a challenge - and are still willing to face it, willing to learn it and ready to go out there and *win* it!

I've had a lot of training in this game. *A lot.*

I know how to protect the ball when I'm tripped, knocked or tackled. I've learned the different strategies of my opposing team. I've studied my "designer" road blocks. I've gotten to know their names, their widths, heights and weights. Oh and I've trained, oh how I've ever trained! Strengthened my knees, my legs, my reflexes and my back. I can dodge left, I can dodge right and I can spin with speed and agility around every person and play.

I've gotten to know my teammates. I've picked them carefully, because unlike so many people tell you, you *can* pick your own teammates. I know them well. I work with them well. Together we are powerful. Together we are a great team. Together, we're able to win.

Life is war. And you know it when you see it, don't you? They wear it clear as day. Whether, at the end of the line, someone has won the game... or not.

I fully intend on winning it. Are you? Then let's get to it. Hands together... (insert some inspiring chant. One that gets you jumpy and pumped...) aaaaaaand - BREAK! It's time to hit the field.

Let's go!

2 THE STADIUM
A NEW KIND OF STAGE

Each of our lives is built just like a stadium is. It's uncanny. We all have a playing field, we all have onlookers and we all have coaches, cheerleaders, etc. And, just like the football stadiums that grace our nation, each one of ours is different. Unique. Built perfectly for our teams.

Your stadium is amazing, majestic and tailored in many ways to you. So is mine. But in the essentials we are the same. And it's the essentials I'm going to lay out for you right now. These are the building blocks upon which our lives are built. Know how to utilize each section wisely and your opposition will find themselves faced with quite the opponent.

First there's your playing field. It's just as large,

dramatic and looming as the ones you see in high definition during the Super Bowl. That long, wide stretch of green grass and turf is the stage upon which your life is lived. Played. Determined.

- Playing the Field -

Every moment you're on that field you want the ball to be in your hands, not the others.' You want to move it towards your goal line, not away from it. And because you will always have an opposing team, you will always need to be ready for them.

In order to win though, you need to be more than just ready. Especially when the stakes are as high as they are - this is your life. You don't want to be some set of stats and the end of your game. Even the worst teams in history have stats. That's not what you're here for.

You need special training to win on that playing field. It can be energizing, lifting and exciting when you're finally winning and playing the game right. But to get there you need to have the right team, the right coaching, the best support system and the most incredible playbook ever. Which you are about to receive.

And once you succeed, you can start aiming for the end zone without fear. Oh yes, our fields have end zones too. And the goal posts. The goal lines. The touchdowns. Oh! The glorious touchdowns! How much more powerful are the touchdowns in our stadiums!

Touchdowns are at the heart of this book. There are

many different kinds, but all of them are important to make. They don't just affect us, but the world around us. It affects our future and it even affects how we view our future. We are built for touchdowns. We are built to win.

When we don't, our bodies know it. The stadium knows it. The atmosphere grows dim. It's hard to come back from a losing streak. But then again, it's hard to stop winning when you are on a winning streak too. So it's time to start winning, asap. And the way we do that is to start making the kind of touchdowns with the greatest impact first.

So many out there tell us to start at the top of the heap that is our lives and slowly dig our way down to the bottom, where the real troubles lay. Or to look at it another way, some people want to trim the tree that is our life - trim it back, further and further until finally you can see the trunk.

And then, once the trunk is exposed, you can trim your way right down to the roots. And once you're finally down to the roots - Oh! - Shocking! - The roots are bad. We'll have to dig them out and replant a new tree. No kidding.

I say we start at the bottom and the rest will follow. I say we heal the roots first and - Hey - The tree will get better! That's just my approach. Much quicker. Deeper-less easy- but wonderfully warm, yet hopeful, with just a touch of giggle in there.

These are the touchdowns we need to make first.

These are the vital goals that, once we hit the scoreboard with them, will turn your game around. Shake up your stadium a bit. Wake everyone up.

It's time to get back to winning again. And how.

- Touchdowns -

Not all touchdowns are equal in our stadiums. The most important ones are built upon the ones that came before them. They require strength that only previous touchdowns can provide. It's the nature of growing. A simple example is our children. They don't just stand up and walk after being held for so long. No, there's a long process of building - taking things step, by step, by step.

I loved seeing this first hand for the first time in my oldest nephew...

READ ON!
OWN YOUR OWN COPY OF TOUCHDOWN!

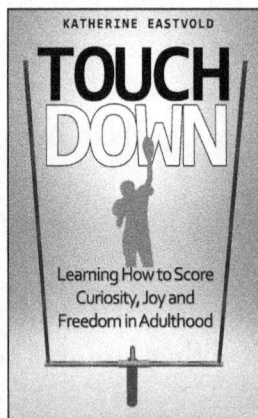

KATHERINE EASTVOLD

TOUCH DOWN

Learning How to Score
Curiosity, Joy and
Freedom in Adulthood

AVAILABLE ON AMAZON.COM

ABOUT THE AUTHOR

Katherine Elizabeth Eastvold is a seasoned author with a background in teaching and speaking. Enjoying 20 years of one-on-one work with K-12 students, adults and corporations, she's developed a loyal following both here in the States and around the world. Her previous work includes three books: *Touchdown: How to Score Curiosity, Joy and Freedom in Adulthood, Telling the Truth* and *Setting Dancers Free.*

FURTHER READING

Touchdown
How to Score Curiosity, Joy and Freedom in Adulthood

Telling the Truth
The Groundbreaking Articles That Saved WCS

Setting Dancers Free
The Weekly Notes That Rocked the World of WCS

EXTERNAL LINKS

Katherine's Website
www.wcskat.com
Read reviews, find great resources, videos & more!

Katherine is also on:

THE COSBY SHOW

All 8 Seasons of *The Cosby Show* are available for purchase on DVD. Instant Streaming of *The Cosby Show* is currently available on Amazon.com and Hulu.com.

DISCLAIMER

Author's opinions are entirely her own. The author shares no affiliation with any party or parties referred to or otherwise mentioned in this book.

www.ingramcontent.com/pod-product-compliance
Lightning Source LLC
Chambersburg PA
CBHW021211020426
42331CB00003B/308

* 9 7 8 0 9 8 8 5 6 0 1 5 4 *